a spring-fed pond

Photographs by
James Baker Hall

published by:

Crystal Communications
2009 Family Circle, Suite 3
Lexington, Kentucky 40505

859-255-0076
crystalky@starband.net

acknowledgements & credits

I want to thank Wendell, Bobbie Ann, Ed, Gurney, and Mary Ann for permission to use these brief passages from their work. And for much else besides, though this is hardly the place for more than an allusion to that.

Over the intense months of work that went into the making of this book, I've grown increasingly fond and respectful of the staff at Crystal Communications in Lexington, Kentucky. They know what they are about, and how to go about it with a combination of good cheer and professionalism that I want to celebrate here. I loved going to their offices and working with them, and knew early on that I was in especially able hands. Bobbie Newman I want to mention by name: she helped save me from blunders in the Foreword and Afterword. And Paula Gron, the designer, whose knowing assistance in sequencing and sizing and placement I came to depend on. And Todd Detering for his expert technical assistance. And Ed Puterbaugh, Crystal's president, without whom *A Spring-Fed Pond* would not have come to be. Among Ed's many smarts is knowing how to work with artists. A champion of this project from the get-go, he's been a master at knowing when and how he could help me.

Also I want to thank Anne Tower of the Tower Gallery in Lexington for guiding me to Crystal Communications, and for her continuing expert advice. Harriet Fowler, the recently retired Director of the University of Kentucky Art Museum, worked hard for the fruition of this project; without her early enthusiasm I doubt you would be reading these words. Rebecca Howell and Arwen Donahue must be acknowledged as well; often I seek out their judgment in aesthetic matters, and not infrequently defer to it.

Thanking Mary Ann for her help in this book is a little too much like trying to thank her for her help in general. Let me here dedicate *A Spring-Fed Pond* to her, in lieu of words adequate to my gratitude. If there's another spirit in the world as beautiful and profound, I've not yet come across it. **JBH**

First printing January 2002

Graphic design by Paula Gron
Copyediting by Bobbie Newman
Photo scans by Erin Puterbaugh
Digital color correction by Todd Detering

Printed in Canada

Library of Congress Control Number: 2001094191
ISBN #0-945738-50-1 (hard-bound)
ISBN #0-945738-52-8 (paperback)

2

foreword

Wendell, Ed, Gurney and I were students together under Robert Hazel at the University of Kentucky in the mid-1950s, with Bobbie following a couple of years behind. Thanks in good measure to Robert's impact on our lives, the four guys all went to Stanford on Stegner Fiction Fellowships, bambambambam, and a kinship of heritage started deepening into a common fate. We were young writers together, which was a big, deep, ongoing deal, hot and quick and then hot and quick again; we were innocents abroad traveling under the same passport, which made us treasured allies; we were ever-closer friends, tied together for life by the mid-60s. Mary Ann came into this picture in the late 70s, when she and I got together, and Bobbie about the same time, when her scholarly writing gave way to fiction, and *The New Yorker* took her up.

When the idea of this book presented itself, following on Director Harriet Fowler and the UK Art Museum's interest in an exhibition, I had to dig and scramble to find out just what negatives had survived, and this took a while. When I finally turned up the one of Gurney charging up out of the ocean with exuberance, such appetite for his life past, present and future manifest in his dear young face, I bolted from my chair in a cheer, realizing that maybe I did have what was needed to make a show—a presiding image for us all, as I see it. And when I began to find proofsheets I didn't remember, and to see the remembered ones through new eyes, I realized that I had more keepers than I expected, and began to imagine a book as well.

That picture of Gurney, and the other early ones of him, were taken in 1960 or thereabouts on the West Coast when he was in his very early twenties, during our time together at Stanford, when we were in the heady company of hot-shots and hot-shots-to-be. The first ones of Bobbie were made in the mid-60s in Storrs, Connecticut, where she was a graduate student at UConn, and we were friends and neighbors. The first of Ed in Corvallis, Oregon, in 1961, when he was in his mid-twenties, the next several years later in his Palo Alto office, down the hall from Gurney's. The early ones of Wendell were made back and forth between Henry County, Kentucky, and the West Coast, beginning I think when he was twenty-two, and the most recent in my Lexington studio a few months ago. Not the first I took of Mary Ann, but the first as arranged here, were made in point of metaphorical fact when she was nine and I was ninety-nine.

3

And so on. We've had a lot to do with one another, all over the place, for a long time. As far as I'm concerned, it won't do to be interested in what's transpired among us and be in a hurry, or be looking for a neat paragraph or chapter of strictly literary history. Our kinship is deep and complex, which means that we're not a school, or a movement, or even a common cause, our cherished heritage and much of our subject matter notwithstanding. The differences between Wendell and Bobbie and the work they've done are far deeper and more compelling and to the point of our interest in them than what they share, literature itself excluded. The same is true for any two of us compared. Thank God, and amen.

Putting words and pictures together was a preoccupation of mine back in the late 60s and early 70s. I tracked down everything I could find that had been done creatively along those lines, and I tried out everything that I could imagine—an experience that sent me searching soon enough for more promising pursuits. There are only a few efforts at words-and-pictures successful enough to follow you around, that's been my experience, with *Let Us Now Praise Famous Men* by Walker Evans and James Agee being the only one widely known. Usually the pictures turn out to be illustrations for the words, or the words captions to the pictures, even when something more lively is intended; and when the die-hard journalistic habit of mind doesn't undercut the enterprise, the failure of the words to be up to the art of the pictures does, or vice versa. If the great fun I've had rereading these authors and selecting these excerpts and placing them means what I think it means, and the elements are as dynamic for others as they are for me, then *A Spring-Fed Pond* has a chance to be an unlikely kind of book.

Once you've checked out the arrangement I settled on, be a guest of the spirit at work here, and try one of your own, or more than one. With your favorite author, move the words around and about among the pictures, and watch and listen to what happens. Better still, bring your own excerpts to the pictures—very short ones, please, take my word for it—and play around with their placement, watching and listening. In the picture is a tip of an iceberg, in the words some of the weight beneath the surface, except when it's the other way around. It's an experience of the eye and ear, not the conceptualizing intellect, as our schooling would make it. Myself, I can't stand it when the words attach themselves too literally to one picture, at the expense of free-floating and the iceberg effect—but that may be just me.

Best of all, read or reread *Divine Right's Trip*, *The Natural Man*, *The Memory of Old Jack*, *Come and Go*, *Molly Snow*, *Clear Springs*. As Ezra Pound observed, "In the gloom, the gold gathers the light against it."

James Baker Hall

James Baker Hall
Harrison County, Kentucky
July 2001

wendell berry

8

9

To his death? Yes.

He walks and sings to his death.

And winter will equal spring.

And for the lovers, even
while they kiss, even though
it is spring, the day ends.

But to the sound of his passing
he sings. It is a kind of triumph
that he grieves—thinking
of the white lilacs in bloom,
profuse, fragrant, white
in excess of all seasonal need,

and of the mockingbird's crooked
arrogant notes, hooking him to the sky
as though no flight
or dying could equal him
at his momentary song.

from "A Man Walking and Singing"
The Broken Ground

Love foresees a jointure
composing a house, a marriage
of contraries, compendium
of opposites in equilibrium.
This morning the sun
came up before the moon set;
shadows were stripped from the house
like burnt rags, the sky turning
blue behind the clear moon,
day and night moving to day.

Let severances be as dividing
budleaves around the flower
—woman and child enfolded, chosen.
It's a dying begun, not lightly,
the taking up of this love
whose legacy is its death.

from "The Design of a House"
Findings

13

14

To be sane in a mad time
is bad for the brain, worse
for the heart. The world
is a holy vision, had we clarity
to see it—a clarity that men
depend on men to make.

from "The Mad Farmer Manifesto:
The First Amendment"
The Country of Marriage

But the man so forcefully walking,
say where he goes,
say what he hears and what he sees
and what he knows
to cause him to stride so merrily.

He goes in spring
through the evening street
to buy bread,

green trees leaning
over the sidewalk,
forsythia yellow
beneath the windows,
birds singing
as birds sing
only in spring,

and he sings, his footsteps
beating the measure of his song.

In an open window
a man and a woman
leaning together
at the room's center
embrace and kiss
as if they met
in passing,
the spring wind
lifting the curtain.

His footsteps carry him
past the window,
deeper into his song.

His singing becomes conglomerate
of all he sees,
leaving the street behind him
runged as a ladder
or the staff of a song.

from "A Man Walking and Singing"
The Broken Ground

And I am here in Kentucky in the place I have made myself
in the world. I sit on my porch above the river that flows muddy
and slow along the feet of the trees. I hear the voices of the wren
and the yellow-throated warbler whose songs pass near the
        windows
and over the roof. In my house my daughter learns the
        womanhood
of her mother. My son is at play, pretending to be
the man he believes I am. I am the outbreathing of this ground.
My words are its words as the wren's song is its song.

from "To a Siberian Woodsman"
Openings

Except in idea, perfection is as wild
as light; there is no hand laid on it.
But the house is a shambles
unless the vision of its perfection
      upholds it like stone.

More probable: the ideal
      of its destruction:
cloud of fire prefiguring
      its disappearance.

What value there is
          is assumed;

like a god, the house elects its omens;
because it is, I desire it should be
—white, its life intact in it,
      among trees.

Love has conceived a house,
and out of its labor
brought forth its likeness
—the emblem of desire, continuing
though the flesh falls away.

from "The Design of a House"
Findings

I am done with apologies. If contrariness is my
inheritance and destiny, so be it. If it is my mission
to go in at exits and come out at entrances, so be it.
I have planted by the stars in defiance of the experts,
and tilled somewhat by incantation and by singing,
and reaped, as I knew, by luck and Heaven's favor,
in spite of the best advice. If I have been caught
so often laughing at funerals, that was because
I knew the dead were already slipping away,
preparing a comeback, and can I help it?

from "The Contrariness of the Mad Farmer"
Farming: A Hand Book

Vision must have severity
at its edge:

      against neglect,
bushes grown over the pastures,
vines riding down
the fences, the cistern broken;

against the false vision
of the farm dismembered,
sold in pieces on the condition
of the buyer's ignorance,
a disorderly town
of "houses in the country"
inhabited by strangers;

against indifference, the tracks
of the bulldozer running
to gullies;

      against weariness,
the dread of too much to do,
the wish to make desire
easy, the thought of rest.

from "The Clearing"
Clearing

I made this book
for my father,
its true source,
in gratitude
and in celebration.

from *The Memory of Old Jack*

41

My life's wave is at its crest.
The thought of work becomes
a friend of the thought of rest.
I see how little avail
one man is, and yet I would not
be a man sitting still,
no little song of desire
traveling the mind's dark woods.

I am trying to teach my mind
to bear the long, slow growth
of the fields, and to sing
of its passing while it waits.

from "From the Crest"
Clearing

43

46

Since before sunup Old Jack has been standing at the edge of the hotel porch, gazing out into the empty street of the town of Port William, and now the sun has risen and covered him from head to foot with light. But not yet with warmth, and in spite of his heavy sheepskin coat he has grown cold. He pays that no mind. When he came out and stopped there at the top of the steps, mindful of the way the weight of his body is taking him, he propped it carefully with his cane and, in the way that has lately grown upon him, left it.

From the barn whose vaned cupola was visible over the house roof against the pale sky, Mat Feltner was calling his cows. Old Jack listened with an eagerness that carried him away from himself; for all his consciousness of where he was, he might have been asleep and dreaming. Mat waited, and called again. And then from the quietening of Mat's voice, Old Jack knew that the cows had come near and that Mat could see them moving up deliberative and shadowy out of the mists and the thinning darkness. And then he heard the barn doors slide open.

from *The Memory of Old Jack*

50

The town's ever-vigilant curiosity, which saw in the dark, found them out. And he did not care. The talk went around under cover of righteousness. And need was the cause of it. The little groups that the talk stirred in the stores and the kitchens and the street were like people lighting torches at a fire. It was as if Jack and Rose, like other lovers before and after them, had been elected to stir from the ashes of pretense and fear the light of a vital flame. And so while it condemned them the town needed them and praised them in the darkness of its heart. The town talked and looked askance, and waited eagerly for more news out of that dark and fragrant garden from which it felt itself in exile. And so this coupling went into the town's mind, to belong to its history and its hope, even against its will. Even as the knowledge of it fades, it remains, an inflection of the heart, troubling and consoling the night watches of lonely husbands and wives like a phrase from a forgotten song.

from *The Memory of Old Jack*

Some days, sitting here on my porch over the river, my memory seems to enclose me entirely. I wander back in my reckoning among all of my own that have lived and died until I no longer remember where I am. And then I lift my head and look about me at the river and the valley, the great, unearned beauty of this place, and I feel the memoryless joy of a man just risen from the grave.

from *Jayber Crow*

I have known no sudden revelations. No stroke of light has ever knocked me blind to the ground. But I know now that even then, in my hopelessness and sorrow, I began a motion of the heart toward my origins. Far from rising above them, I was longing to sink into them until I would know the fundamental things. I needed to know the original first chapter of the world.

from *Jayber Crow*

Then, in the loss of all the world, when I might have said the words I had so long wanted to say, I could not say them. I saw that I was not going to be able to talk without crying, and so I cried. I said, "But what about this other thing?"

She looked at me then. "Yes," she said. She held out her hand to me. She gave me the smile that I had never seen and will not see again in this world, and it covered me all over with light.

from *Jayber Crow*

bobbie ann
mason

Steve leaves the supermarket and hits the sunlight. Blinking, he stands there a moment, then glances at his feet. He has on running shoes, but he was sure he had put on boots. He touches his face. He hasn't shaved. His car, illegally parked in the space for the handicapped, is deep blue and wicked. The rear has "Midnight Magic" painted on it in large pink curlicue letters with orange-and-red tails. Rays of color, fractured rainbows, spread out over the flanks. He picked the design from a thick book the custom painters had. The car's rear end is hiked up like a female cat in heat. Prowling in his car at night, he could be Dracula.

Sitting behind the wheel, he eats the chocolate-covered doughnuts he just bought and drinks from a carton of chocolate milk. The taste of the milk is off. They do something weird to chocolate milk now. His father used to drive a milk truck, before he got arrested for stealing a shipment of bowling shoes he found stacked up behind a shoe store. He had always told Steve to cover his tracks and accentuate the positive.

from "Midnight Magic"
Love Life

"I've only knowed two women in my life that I could get out coon hunting," the man in the blue cap said.

"This lady claims she wants a bird dog, but I think I can make a coon hunter out of her," said Buddy, grinning at Ruby.

The man walked away, hunched over a cigarette he was lighting, and Buddy Landon started to sing "You Ain't Nothin' But A Hound Dog." He said to Ruby, "I could have been Elvis Presley. But thank God I wasn't. Look what happened to him. Got fat and died." He sang, " 'Crying all the time. You ain't never caught a rabbit . . .' I love dogs. But I tell you one thing. I'd never let a dog in the house. You know why? It would get too tame and forget its job. Don't forget, a dog is a dog."

Buddy took Ruby by the elbow and steered her through the fairgrounds, guiding her past tables of old plastic toys and kitchen utensils. "Junk," he said. He bought Ruby a Coke in a can, and then he bought some sweet corn from a farmer. "I'm going to have me some roastin' ears tonight," he said.

"I hear your dogs calling for you," said Ruby, listening to the distant bugle voices of the beagles.

"They love me. Stick around and you'll love me too."

"What makes you think you're so cute?" said Ruby. "What makes you think I need a dog?"

He answered her questions with a flirtatious grin. His belt had a large silver buckle, with a floppy-eared dog's head engraved on it. His hands were thick and strong, with margins of dirt under his large, flat nails. Ruby liked his mustache and the way his chin and the bill of his cap seemed to yearn toward each other.

"How much do you want for that speckled hound dog?" she asked him.

from "Third Monday"
Shiloh and Other Stories

70

I didn't want to spend my life canning beans and plucking chickens, so trundling my innocence before me like a shopping cart, I headed for New York—where else?—and got a job on a movie magazine. But I wasn't a glamour-puss, I hated cocktail parties, and writing celebrity gossip soon palled. I wanted to be a real writer, which I thought meant I had to become a Greenwich Village bohemian. I didn't know that the postwar portrait of the Village artist was already turning into a caricature. Bob Dylan—Nick Carroway's country cousin—had arrived in the Village some time before, not as a starry-eyed tourist like me but as a revolutionary messenger from the boondocks. But it was a long time before I understood how Dylan affirmed the very resources I had left behind.

from *Clear Springs*

Finally, the fish was at the bank, its mouth shut on the line like a clamp-top canning jar, its whiskers working like knitting needles. It was enormous. She was astonished. It touched the bank, but without the smooth glide of the water to support it the fish was dead weight. She couldn't pull it all the way up the bank. She couldn't lift it with her rod, nor could she drag it through the weeds of the bank. She was more worn out than the fish was, she thought. She held the line taut, so that the fish couldn't slip back in the water, and she tugged, but it didn't give. The mud was sucking it, holding it fast. Its head was out of the water, and with those whiskers and its wide wraparound mouth, it seemed to be smiling at her. She stepped carefully through scrubby dried weeds and clumps of grass, making her way down the shallow bank toward the fish. Knots of pondweed bordered the water. Gingerly, she placed her left foot on a patch of dried vegetation and reached toward the fish.

The patch appeared solid. For a fraction of a second, the surprise of its give was like the strangeness of the taste of Coca-Cola when the tongue had expected iced tea. The ground gave way under her foot and she slid straight into the pond. It wasn't a hard fall, for her weight slid right into the water, almost gracefully. On the way, she grabbed at a willow bush but missed it. She still had hold of the line, even though her rod-and-reel slipped into the water. She clutched at dried weeds as she slid, and the brittle leaves crumpled in her hands. Then the fish was slipping back into the water, dragging the rod. She snatched the rod and felt the fish still weighting the end of the line. Quickly, she heaved the rod to the bank. She caught hold of the fish and held it tight, her fingernails studding its skin.

from *Clear Springs*

In the Wal-Mart parking lot, he has a sudden queasy feeling. He can't remember where he is. He sees rows and rows of cars. His brain reels. He must have a car here, but he can't remember what car. He sees a Camaro, an Oldsmobile, rows of shiny silver and white cars, lined up like teeth. The vertical lines of street lamps tower in the landscape like defoliated trees. The parking lot seems slightly familiar, but he can't place it. He may be thinking of one he has seen on TV. He stumbles onward and suddenly spots his car—the Rabbit that needs a tune-up. The little car seems to have aged ten years overnight. It is parked next to a black van with round windows and a pink-and-blue mural of an angel and a Jesus with a halo. Spence wonders what loony drives such a vehicle. Spence has never been comfortable in church. He is suspicious of most preachers and believes all the evangelists on the radio and TV are con artists. The night before, when Lila came out of the recovery room and was wheeled back into Room 301, she said to him, "Did you pray for me?" Her question startled him. They never spoke of prayer, or heaven, but Spence knew she prayed for him, frequently, because she went to church and was afraid that because he didn't they wouldn't end up in heaven together. When he answered her, he felt a chill up his spine. "Sure," he said, joking. "You know how good I am at saying grace." She got tickled at him then but had to stop laughing because she hurt. "I've got a long row to hoe," she said. She wasn't fully awake.

from *Spence and Lila*

"She's been after me about those strawberries till I could wring her neck," says Mother as she and Nancy are getting ready for bed. "She's talking about some strawberries she put up in nineteen seventy-*one*. I've told her and told her that she eat them strawberries back then, but won't nothing do but for her to have them strawberries."

"Give her some others," Nancy says.

"She'd know the difference...."

from "Nancy Culpepper"
Shiloh and Other Stories

"I'll give you one of these crazies when you stop moving around," Opal says. "You couldn't fit it in that backpack of yours." She polishes her glasses thoughtfully. "Do you know what those quilts mean to me?"

"No, what?"

"A lot of desperate old women ruining their eyes. Do you know what I think I'll do?"

"No, what?"

"I think I'll take up aerobic dancing. Or maybe I'll learn to ride a motorcycle. I try to be modern."

"You're funny, Aunt Opal. You're hilarious."

"Am I gorgeous, too?"

"Adorable," says Jenny.

from title story of
Love Life

91

...He pulls up to the side of a gas station, in front of the telephone booth. He leaves the motor running and feels in his pocket for a quarter. He flips the quarter, thinking heads. It's tails. There are emergency numbers on the telephone. The emergency numbers are free. He pockets the quarter and dials. A recorded voice asks him to hold.

In a moment, a woman's voice answers. Steve answers in a tone higher than normal. "I was driving south on I-24? And I want to report that I saw a man laying on the side of the road. I don't know if he was dead or just resting."

"Where are you, sir?"

"Now? Oh, I'm at a gas station."

"Location of gas station?"

"Hell, I don't know. The Clarksville exit."

"North or south?"

"South. I said south."

"What's the telephone number you're speaking from?"

He spreads his free hand on the glass wall of the telephone booth and gazes through his fingers at pie-slice sections of scenery. Up on the interstate, the traffic proceeds nonchalantly, as indifferent as worms working the soil. The woman's voice is asking something else over the phone. "Sir?" she says. "Are you there, sir?" His head buzzes from the beer. On his knuckle is a blood blister he doesn't know where he got.

Steve studies his car through the door of the phone booth. It's idling, jerkily, like a panting dog. It speeds up, then kicks down. His muffler has been growing throatier, making an impressive drag-race rumble. It's the power of Midnight Magic, the sound of his heart.

from "Midnight Magic"
Love Life

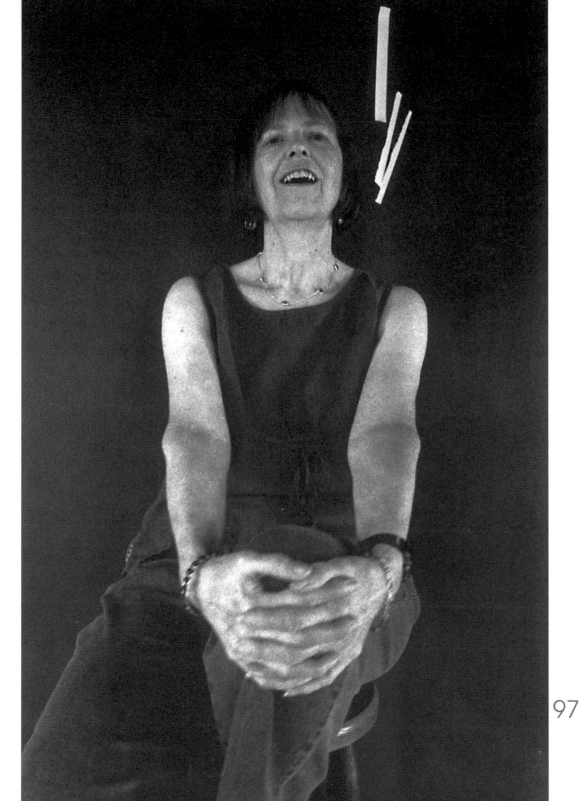

ed
mcclanahan

103

Larry, the honcho of the construction outfit I was working for, was such a cheapskate he wouldn't buy us hard hats. He'd contracted to dismantle a four-story steel storage shed, and one day early that summer, he dropped a one-inch steel nut and bounced it off my head from forty feet above. If he'd sneaked up behind me and rapped me sharply on the noggin with a ball-peen hammer, it couldn't have been more effective. I went down like I'd been shot, and a few minutes later when I came to, with a halo of little cuckoo birds circling my head, I was already reassessing my career options. Within the next few days, I was at the University of Kentucky in Lexington, registering for a couple of graduate English lit summer school classes.

from *My Vita, If You Will*

Down at the end of the block, where Hanover meets Page Mill, some kind of rumble is in progress; over the heads of the crowd I can see revolving blue gumball-machine lights, and people are craning for a look. Behind me, a woman screams. I hear the muffled *whumpf* of what is, I will realize momentarily, the launching of the first tear-gas grenade. It lands on the street somewhere off to my right—*thwok*—at the fringes of the crowd. More screams, more *whumpfs*, more *thwoks*. My first thought is to seek what I imagine to be the relative safety of the peaceful protester ranks, but I reach the street in time to see those good souls disband in wild disarray, a hissing, fuming grenade having just landed *thwok* amidst them, like a missive from Old Man Hate himself. So much for the soft-answer defense.

from *My Vita, If You Will*

"O-o-o-o-kiiii-naaaa-waaaaaaaa!" the Head intones at last. "O-o-o-kiii-naaa-waaa!"

Wade looks to the professor for an interpretation and meets with a *no comprende* shrug; the Man of Letters purports to be as mystified as Wade is. And when Wade looks back, the Head is gone, withdrawn into its hole again. On the platter is the empty turban, a wadded dish towel in a pool of painted blood.

"That's all?" Wade asks in disbelief.

"That's it, son," says the professor, not unkindly. "That's the whole shit-a-ree, as it were."

"Well, it's all a big gyp, then."

"That's as may be," admits the professor, holding back the exit flap for him. "But you must never presume upon the cosmos, my lad. That wouldn't be...good policy."

from *A Congress of Wonders*

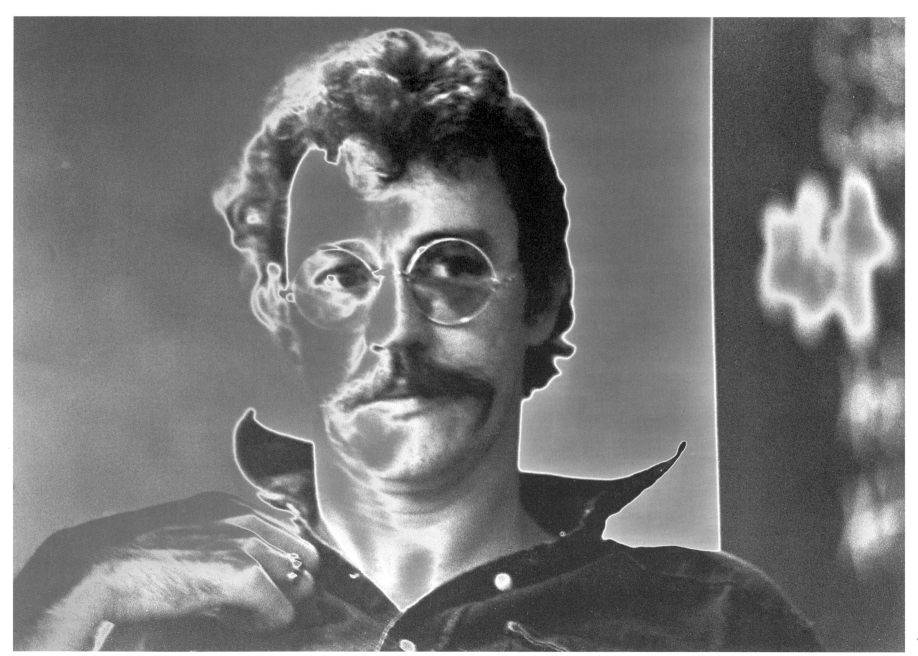

113

We are all on our feet now, and the Beast is shaking my hand again, and Wheatgerm and Yogurt are sort of plucking at my sleeves, imploring me one last time to forgive them for ripping off such a hip dude. And I, of course, am doing so with all my heart, trailing them halfway down the front hall dispensing absolution, feeling guilty as sin for stealing back my typewriter. For want of something better to offer them in recompense for the injustice of it all, I mention that I might try to write something about them sometime.

"Good fucking deal, man," the Beast says heartily. "You can write anything you want to about me. 'Cause I can't read anyhow."

from *Famous People I Have Known*

118

Wherever we took the bus, from the shopping mall in Roseburg, Oregon to the streets of Berkeley, it was greeted by smiles of recognition, honking horns, upraised fists, and more V signs (okay, peace signs, if you insist) than I'd seen in twenty years. On a cold, windy weekday midnight, in the parking lot of a convenience store on the outskirts of Weed, California, it instantly drew a crowd of admirers; in Portland and Berkeley and San Francisco and Palo Alto, it drew sweet, mild-mannered little mobs. Even to those unfamiliar with its fossilology, Furthur seemed—seems—almost immediately to suggest personal liberation, artistic freedom, gaiety, joy; everywhere one sensed an almost palpable wonder in the air, and felt oneself present at the rebirth of a frail, nascent kind of hope.

from *Famous People I Have Known*

It was an exhilarating time to be at Stanford. The antiwar movement and the civil rights movement and the Free University movement and the hippie movement and what we might call, in retrospect, the General, All-Purpose Up-Yours Movement were all flourishing, and I was ardently attached to each and every one. By the midsixties, I was industriously insinuating myself into every sit-in and teach-in and be-in and love-in that happened along. I was also going around the campus in a knee-length red velvet cape, accessorized with a mod-bob haircut and granny glasses and Peter Pan boots. "Captain Kentucky," I styled myself, while Daniel Boone turned over in his grave.

from *My Vita, If You Will*

Harry was not athletically inclined. The reason he'd settled on sportswriting as his calling was simply that he loved the Vernacular of the Game—that rich, mellifluous language in which the scribes of the playing field alone are privileged to express themselves; loved the way that, on the sports page, some stalwart is forever sizzling the twines or knocking the hide off the spheroid or booting the oval or pilfering the sacks; loved the assonance, the alliteration, the sheer mythmaking hyperbole, the splendid excess of it all, the poetry!

from *The Natural Man*

Alone again, Harry sets down his attaché case and goes back into the inner lobby. The door to the box office hangs from one hinge; he wrestles it aside and enters the little booth. At first he thinks the speaking tube is gone. Then he sees that it has been torn loose from the wall and twisted upward, like the tendril of a living plant turning its bloom to the light. He pulls it down and brings it to his lips.

"Are you ready up there?" he whispers urgently. "Are you ready up there?"

Though he waits a long time, no answer is forthcoming. But that doesn't really matter, Harry tells himself—for the show goes on, because it must.

from *The Natural Man*

127

"And now, my sons," the reverend declaimed after their first few miles on the road, waving his unlit stogie at the windshield as though he were conducting a symphony of himself, "let us take sweet counsel together. Why do the heathen rage, you ask? I'll tell you why, my lads. Because the way of the transgressor is hard! Because the serpent abideth in the garden! Because the king of terrors stalks the earth, while Hell enlarges itself daily! Yea, verily, I have seen all Israel scattered upon the hills, as sheep that have not a shepherd, and doubtless there are those among them that wouldn't pay a nickel to see a pissant eat a bale of hay! But *we* shall shepherd them, Luther my boy! Together, you and I shall drive the wolf from the fold and teach the children of Israel that above all things, the Lord loveth a cheerful giver!"

128

And while I'm asking questions, I'll ask these: Were the Stonebreaker girls all watching from the stoop when my egg burst like a de Kooning masterpiece inside the Rambler? Did they scream and squeal like bobby-soxers when this miracle of art and magic and athletic prowess transpired right before their very eyes? Did Bernice and I go to the movies that night—the sit-down movies, not the drive-in—and did I, when I took her home afterward, kiss her on the lips on that very stoop?

No, sports fans, I'm afraid not, I'm afraid not. But...O the clear moment!

from *My Vita, If You Will*

His purpose in life, Finch saw now all too clearly, was to provide, by his sufferings, for the amusement and diversion of his fellow-man. By little and little, Finch's dread of his departure from this mortal coil had almost entirely given way to a deep, inchoate longing to begin the journey, a longing not so much to die as merely to be...elsewhere, to be taken, to join those shadowy legions known as The Departed.

134

137

Atop the courthouse, that imposing eyesore, is situated yet another imposing eyesore: a bulbous, beehive-shaped cupola with four clock faces the size of mill wheels, each asserting with all the authority of its hugeness four entirely different times of day. Two sides of the clock have, in fact, long since concluded that being right twice a day is better than never being right at all and have taken their stands at, respectively, 9:14 and 7:26. The remaining pair toil on, not in tandem but quite independently, one gaining several seconds every hour, the other just as resolutely losing them. There is, moreover, a bell in the clock tower that has a timetable all its own and is liable to toll midnight at three in the morning and noon at suppertime. The dedicated public servants in the courthouse learned long ago to ignore altogether the two broken clocks and the bell and to come to work by the slow clock and knock off by the fast one. They regard their singular timepiece as a labor-saving device and treasure it accordingly.

138

gurney
norman

Bulldozers pushed the tops of the mountains into the valleys so they could scoop the coal up with machines. About eighty per cent of my grandfather's farm here is under mud now, and out behind the house there's this incredible big mound of mud, this big wall of it, about fifteen feet high, waiting on a rain to loosen it enough to flow right on through this very kitchen. I wish you could see it.

from *Divine Right's Trip*

Wilgus came forward and without hesitation took the money, visions of spending it already forming in his mind. He'd buy watermelons with it. He'd host the entire family at a watermelon feast, outside in the yard. He'd jump in Delmer's Ford and run down to Godsey's store and get four of those big ripe melons just in from Georgia, and they would all gather in the yard and feast on them before they set out for their various destinations later in the day.

But that was a romantic vision, and terribly timed. His relatives had no patience for any watermelon feast this Memorial Day. Hastily they gathered up their children and piled into their cars, Wilgus among them as they drove down the Trace Fork road to the highway.

That's okay, Wilgus thought as he drove alone toward Lexington. There's other things to do with money. He would spend it on beer at the Paddock Club, share his windfall with his writer friends. And as they drank, he would tell them about his family in the hills, describe Memorial Day weekend with the clan. His friends might not believe the stories about his family, but still they would join him in a toast to their benefactors. "To the clan!" Wilgus would say, holding his glass aloft. And his pals would clink their glasses and drink together, and then say, "To the clan!"

from "Home for the Weekend"
Kinfolks

148

It was nearly dark by the time they got to where they'd left the tools and wire. And by the time they got back to the barn, full night had come. Wilgus stood outside while his grandfather went in the barn to put the tools away. Across the dark back yard he saw the lighted windows of the house. There in the kitchen was his grandmother, standing by the stove. *Grandma*, Wilgus thought. *There she is.* And when his grandfather came out of the barn and the two of them started walking together toward the house he thought: *Grandad. Here he is.* And there it was again: a feeling, deep inside, trying to occur, an idea that Wilgus would be a long time knowing. But that was okay. Let it take its time. He was a patient man. Just knowing that one day he would know was quite enough for now.

from "The Favor"
Kinfolks

Delmer pulled up in front of his mother's house and blew the horn.

His nephew Wilgus came running out the back door carrying his jacket in his hand.

The boy's grandmother chased him through the back door and across the porch yelling, "Wilgus! Wilgus! You listen to me!"

But by the time she reached the steps the boy was already climbing into his uncle's car.

"You be careful with that child!" she yelled to Delmer.

"See you later!" Delmer yelled back laughing.

The gravel flew as he wheeled his Ford around and scratched off down the hill toward the county road.

from "Night Ride"
Kinfolks

...I recognized the shape of the figure in the water as my own. But the figure was a stranger too who moved in mysterious ways. The figure moved like a woman moves. When I lifted my hand the figure lifted its hand. I began to dance with this woman of the water, I moved on the rocky shore while she moved with me in the water. I raised my hand. She raised her hand. I shifted my feet and turned. The woman turned. I bowed low and most elegantly, and she bowed too. Our faces were nearly touching. I brought my arms around in a swoop and she did too until our hands were nearly touching. Then my hands sank into the water to the wrists; instantly the ash washed away and my hands drew my entire body into the water, I plunged head first into the pool and swam, down, reaching deep, turning over and over in the cold river. The ash washed off like dust. I turned in the water, I turned again, I was a fish. I had no need to breathe, no urge to leave the water. The water was my habitat, I lay suspended in it, running my hands over my body, feeling my own flesh and delighting in it. My arms felt like a woman's arms, my stomach, legs, everywhere upon me I could feel was like a woman. I looked around for the woman I had seen in the water.

from *Crazy Quilt*

153

There were at least three things the Lone Outdoorsman could have done in response to the filthy crime he saw happen on the big rock by the river. He could have shot big holes in the young couple's arms and legs and heads and backs with his .357 magnum pistol. Or he could have gone to his camper, got his rubber life raft out of his fourteen-foot Cris-Craft motorboat, launched it a mile upstream and staged an amphibious assault upon the little beach near the rocks and captured them before they knew what was happening. Or— and admittedly this is a big or; it's big because, as it turns out, the Lone Outdoorsman is far from your ordinary, everyday one-dimensional heavy; the thing that redeems the Lone Outdoorsman is a refreshing mental complexity of a kind you don't ordinarily run into in folk tales. All mixed in with his gory mental images of bullet-riddled bodies and heroic assaults upon beachheads was a commendable impulse to be nice to these kids, to befriend them and hopefully influence them in some constructive way. In short, the Lone Outdoorsman could either shoot these kids, assault them from the river and take them captive, or else be a good neighbor and invite Divine Right and Estelle over to his place for supper.

And so when D.R. and Estelle had finished balling, had dressed and folded the serape and walked back through the darkening campground to their own scene, they found the Lone Outdoorsman leaning against Urge's front, waiting for them.

from *Divine Right's Trip*

156

I've been having so many thoughts here lately I can't hardly keep it all straight in my mind. It's a workout, trying to keep up with all this I'm thinking. I try to write it down but all I write is bare bones. Blanche fusses at me for scattering paper all over the house. She says I've got to quit my messing and gomming if I'm going to live with her. I need you to help me keep it all straight.

There's many parts of my life I ain't even remembered yet. But there's many that I have, the main ones being 1. working with my daddy in thirty inch coal when I was fourteen years old 2. joining the CCC in 1938 and working in the logwoods in Oregon till 1939 3. working for wages in a copper mine in Butte, Montana six months in 1939 4. coming home to teach the fourth and fifth grades in 1940 when Bonnett Creek School was out of a teacher 5. joining the Army and fighting in New Guinea in 1943, getting a splinter in my head that same year 6. going in the nightclub business after the war here at home and making a lot of money and then losing it all when I got in trouble with the law (1948-1950) 7. meeting and marrying Dorsie Brumley and joining the church and running for the school board in 1950 8. then spending the rest of my life operating a taxi company between here and Hazard till Dorsie died and I had a stroke, both in 1980.

from Crazy Quilt

Listen, I said with some heat. Hiss all you like. But in Western Kentucky there's this big coal-digging machine, three stories tall, with *jaws*, man, that eats whole truck-loads of ground at a bite. It's got legs! It *walks*, man, for twenty years it's been walking on this certain piece of ground, around and around, eating dirt and scooping up coal to heat and light the nation. Gradually the machine has dug a hole three hundred feet deep and a quarter-mile square around the rims of its pit. Finally the coal in that particular spot is gone. And after twenty years, the machine itself is done for, too. Parts worn, design obsolete, there it sits at the bottom of its pit, and they can't get it out! It would cost the company more than the thing is worth to dismantle it and take it out so what's the company going to do? *Leave* it there, that's what. Bury it where it quit. Think about it.

from *Crazy Quilt*

The only mail in the whole batch that was the least bit personal was a post card to Wendell Hall from his daughter in Detroit, and she was asking for money. Mrs. Back's copy of *The Upper Room* came, and Barry Berry got a statement from the Famous Writer's School. Old Mr. McClanahan got a brown envelope from the Social Security Administration but you could tell just by looking that it didn't have a check in it.

162

from *Divine Right's Trip*

163

This drunk woman in the Finley Inn comes by the table where I'm sitting, leans over and sticks her face up close to mine, says, 'There ain't gonna be no hidin' place when God sets the world on fire!'
I know it honey, I say to her. I know it.

from *Crazy Quilt*

165

167

"Excuse me," said D.R. "How much are those fuses there?" He was looking at a sign above a box of fuses that said, "Why be helpless when fuses blow? A few cents spent for a box of fuses will save you possible delay or danger later on."

"Do which?" said the attendant in a high, nasal, hillbilly whine. He was busy making coffee on a hot plate over by the road maps.

"Those fuses. How much are they?"

"Twenty cents apiece," said the attendant.

"Good," said D.R. "I'll take four."

The attendant picked out four fuses and stepped with them to the cash register, yawning as he rang them up. It was about five in the morning, barely sunrise. It was hard to tell if this was an all-night station or the start of a brand-new day.

As the attendant pecked the various keys, D.R. felt a deep sense of well-being glowing inside him. Eighty cents from eighteen eighty left eighteen exactly. How perfect, how balanced, how lovely the word *exactly*. Ex. Act. After the act. It reminded D.R. of the *I Ching* hexagram called After Completion, the one about the importance of tuning the flame beneath the kettle exactly right, so that it burns with a precise intensity. Precision, D.R. thought. Precision and intensity. Those are the keys.

"That'll be eighty-three cents," said the attendant, yawning again.

D.R. looked at him. "How much?"

"Eighty-three cents."

"Why the three cents?" D.R. asked, and when the attendant said sales tax D.R. thought: fucked in the ass by a tax.

D.R was not enlightened by any of this experience, but it edged him a little further along the way.

from *Divine Right's Trip*

168

There was so much junk on the seat and the floor the boy barely found room for himself, and that was on the point of a spring sticking through the cotton wadding and imitation leather of the seat. Around him were tools and parts of two or three old motors, a chainsaw and a can of gasoline, some steel cable and a great coil of thick rope on the floor. The boy glanced at the man curiously, then out at the sky again. Finally he settled back with his feet propped on a tool box.

"Well, what is it?" the fat man asked.

"What's what?" asked Wilgus.

"Your name. What is it? Puddintane?"

"Wilgus Collier," said the boy.

"How was that again?" said the man. He cupped his hand to his ear and leaned in Wilgus' direction. "This old truck makes so much noise I don't hear good."

"Wilgus Collier."

The fat man nodded. "Monroe Short. That's what I thought you said. But I wonder if that's actually right. I mean, could your name be Short Monroe and you just got confused?"

Wilgus grinned. "My name's Wilgus Collier," he said.

"Just like that, eh? Monroe Short and that's all?"

from "Fat Monroe"
Kinfolks

"Give me the hose," said Bert of the Crosstown Rivals. Bert's rival, Norton, had been sucking on the laughing gas almost two minutes now, and Bert was getting antsy. His last flash had been all about time, it had taken him down the passageway to the very door of the rose garden, but as he was about to go in the flash had started to wear off. Against his will he'd come reeling up the same passage he had taken down, and that was a disappointment. If he could have gotten the gas hose when he was supposed to, he could have made it back down in time to keep the dream intact, for even though he'd become conscious again the footprints still echoed clearly in his memory and showed the way back to the garden. But stupid Norton had the greeds and wouldn't let go of the hose.

"Give me the goddamn hose!" said Bert. He reached to take it out of Norton's hand, but Norton, although he was unconscious by now, held it in a slobbery death grip, and Bert was too stoned to fight him. As usual City Girl had to mediate. Gently she worked Norton's hands loose and gave the hose to Bert as Norton fell over in City Girl's lap. Bert put the hose in his mouth and inhaled until he flashed. He wanted the rose garden again, but all he got was Billy Graham silently rapping at him on the top left television screen.

from *Divine Right's Trip*

I remember you, my father, lying through this wall of earth above my head. You played the guitar and sang and drove us around. I remember seeing you carrying groceries on your shoulder in a box, and one time on the courthouse lawn in Hyden eating crackers and sardines and drinking Pepsi-Cola, the two of us there together. Now you are bones and I am bones, and let the dead bones lie. Old fish that used to swim here have no names. Old cows that used to pasture here forgotten, without names. And people that used to live here, Indians in the rockhouses, digging hominy holes, dead, and only remnants of their living here remain. And no names. A few names fading in the headstones maybe, stones already sinking, leaning, eager to lie down. I am lying down.

from *Divine Right's Trip*

183

mary ann taylor-hall

One main sound. It made sense, it figured. There's one main light in the world; everything we call color is a splitting apart of this light. So I thought there might be one great chord, too, like the light of the sun, that separates into the notes of the world. Creation would be the splitting apart of this chord. Music would come out of it, every note, every harmony. Music would also try to get back to it.

It was just an idea, but the idea excited me. I seemed to know what it meant; it drew me. It comforted me.

I didn't hear the sound, not that night. The next night I did—just for a moment, but I was sure of what I heard. A way-off steady chord, a full, low G major, I'd say. Resonant and harmonic.

Then that was what I did. It was my work. Listening. I latched onto the idea of it.

I would come home from Justice's, or wherever, at night. I would undress in the dark and put on my bathrobe and sit against the cool plaster, listening, till the light came.

from Come and Go, Molly Snow

But I always kept my plan right in front of me. I had a realistic view of my assets. What I had going for me was a certain amount of talent, I didn't know how much yet, quick wits, bold good looks, and, for a while anyway, borrowing power up to ten grand. I figured it was only a matter of time till some established band picked me up. I'd already won prizes at a couple of old-time fiddlers' contests, up against some real pros.

And people were beginning to know my name.

194

195

She didn't have any pictures of herself as a child, but later on, after work sometimes, she would pose in the photo booth at the dime store, in her shingled haircut with the finger waves set in, or her plaid wool dress with the fancy white collar. Nobody took her picture so she took her own, smiling in her new velvet beret at some imaginary sweetheart. A thin girl with big sad brown eyes. Not meant to live alone. Gilbert had found these little snapshots, the size of postage stamps, and pasted them all on one page of the photograph album he started when they got married. At the bottom of the page he wrote, "Ten Good Reasons for Coming to Chicago."

She'd gotten what she'd prayed for. They'd had their long life together, three wonderful children. They'd had good times together, sometimes. He'd cheated on her, but he came back and begged her to forgive him. She took him back.

But she never forgave him. Couldn't forgive and couldn't let go, either. Took him back, but kept up her savings account, just in case.

He wouldn't leave. They'd be together for the rest of their lives. In the empty house, she made herself a stiff bourbon and water and drank it at the kitchen sink, then poured herself another little jigger, so she would sleep this time, and took it into the bedroom. She sat back against the pillows, sipping it. Maybe it could be funny now, though it hadn't been funny at the time. A banana boat. You really had to laugh. Poor lying Gilbert, poor dumb scared Rosa, so long ago. Now they were old and still together, hooray—one with no mind, the other crazy.

from "Banana Boats"
How She Knows What She Knows about Yo-Yos

Only when Cap and I sang in harmony, something happened. Our two voices—well, they sounded good together. They slid together trustfully, they were of one mind. The harmony was all instinct, his voice just found the right place for itself against mine, through every last little edgy turn. Harmony's all there is or needs to be, when it's right. It was like dancing. Or worse.

Old footstomper. I gave him something to stomp his foot *about*.

I began to think of Cap pretty near all the time, my unmentionable disease, no matter what else I was doing. Molly was the melody at the top. But Cap was the drone, the ground bass, at the bottom.

Hopeless, is what it was—I didn't want anyone but him; he seemed to want everyone but me, a situation that took up all my nervous energy.

I tried to stop; we both kept it under control, but our eyes were like children or dogs that wouldn't always mind. There was that time, about six months after I started with Hawktown, when we were setting up for a gig in some high school auditorium down in Western Kentucky. We backed into each other, and turned at the same moment—these accidents will happen—and his intent glance touched me like a hand. It might as well have been on bare skin. I felt myself getting ready for liftoff. He met my eyes then, blushing hard, not denying anything, smiling down at me with his deep-end desperate blue eyes. Then he reached out, sort of in spite of himself, to put his right hand in my wild hair, and pulled me toward his shoulder. "Oh good God, Carrie," he said, in a low, unwilling voice.

from Come and Go, Molly Snow

198

199

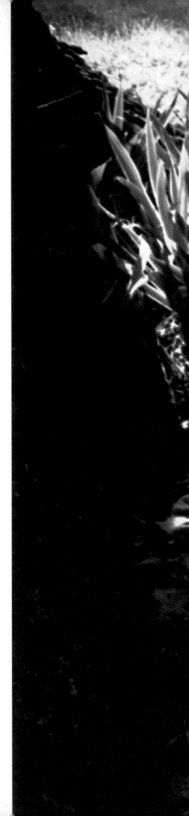

The day after I graduated from high school, I cut out. Left my mama weeping in the carport. "I'll be back, honey, don't cry," I yelled out the window of my inheritance, Daddy's old Riviera. But she knew what I meant: back for Christmas, back for the Shorter family reunion. In all other respects, goodbye flat dirt and frozen-out orange groves, hello I-75. If you want to play the fiddle in a bluegrass band, that's one of the roads you'll *be* on. Renfro Valley to Dayton, Ohio. Live Oak, Florida, to Knoxville, Tennessee. "Doin' 75 on I-75" is the name of a song I wrote that day, on my way to what I mistakenly thought was the bluegrass music capital of the world, Lexington, Kentucky.

from Come and Go, Molly Snow

204

She wanted to stay. Her only physical attachment now was to the things that surrounded her here. The woodstove, for instance. One day, as the fall came in earnest, she found herself standing with her arms around the stovepipe—not touching it, of course, but meaning some kind of embrace, overcome by its faithfulness, its dear silent companionship, the way it kept putting out gentle heat long after she had left the room. On the side of the stove was a motto, in Norwegian, meaning something like: *I pray to God that my fire never goes out.*

from "Advanced Beginners"
How She Knows What She Knows About Yo-Yos

212

I've got to make a plan.
A hot-pink T-shirt ain't a plan.

from *Come and Go, Molly Snow*

She didn't look back. If she had, she knew what she would have seen—the golden chapel on Aldercombe Hill, facing the sea for six centuries. Let it be safe six centuries more, she prayed. Though no light will shine from its tower again, to guide ships through this dying sea. Let it stand somehow, anyhow.

But she didn't look back; it was all turning to photographs now. She'd seen enough. She'd seen what she had been obliged to see. And what she'd wanted to see. She turned north now, up the ridge, and then over it, on the way to Black Grange, to London, to Heathrow, and then to America, her own random country, the New World.

from "The World's Room"
How She Knows What She Knows About Yo-Yos

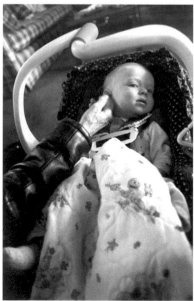

She's not going to think about it any more. She's got her own plan to work out. She means to drive off and leave all the people who knew her in her plaid days. The old tick, tick of the kitchen clock. The half-built wall. Her vision of the future still holds: she wants to see the country, only not with Slip Finnigan. And not in her truck that was her most prized possession. She hopes whatever old wreck Hunter Wurley unloads on her will hold up long enough to get her to somewhere good. Once she gets there, she's got her quick wits and business sense to rely on. She still has assets—what's left in the bank, and this house here and all its contents. The Good Times Express might yet roll. Maybe, by the time the house sells, she'll know something good to do with her money.

She'll go on practicing yo-yos, getting better and better, in her free time when she's not driving the UPS truck. One day when she least expects it, she'll call the yo-yo number. When her yo-yos come in, she'll carry them out to some state park or campground near wherever she ends up. She'll start throwing double walk the dogs, her green yo-yo in one hand, her gold in the other. Maybe a crowd will start forming.

And when she's got them interested, when she's got them where she wants them, she'll lay her round the world on them. Whoosh! Zing! She'll give them a show.

She thinks she can do it. She's a natural for the sport. She's a born athlete.

from title story of
How She Knows What She Knows About Yo-Yos

When she was five or six, she stole a ride on a bread wagon—they all did it, in her neighborhood. But that time, the wagon didn't stop at Mr. Vronka's store, where it usually did. It kept right on moving, turning corners, until she gave up hope. She hung on for dear life as it carried her away from her neighborhood. She didn't dare jump off. When it finally stopped, she was in a part of town she'd never seen. She stood on the curb, crying, while the bread man yelled at her. She didn't understand that she was lost and could be taken back where she came from. She thought just the opposite—that where she came from was lost, the way you might lose a ball or a doll, forever. The bread man took her to the police station. Her knees shook—she thought they would lock her in jail for stealing the ride, but they took her home. At home, they hadn't missed her yet.

from "Banana Boats"
How She Knows What She Knows About Yo-Yos

224

When she's got herself ready, she slips on her flip-flops and goes down the steps into the backyard, hikes herself onto the wall, and swings her legs over it. She practices for a while on her own with her green yo-yo. She's saving the gold one for good. All she can do so far is throw it down and yank it back up into her palm.

After the heaviness of rocks, the yo-yo feels like a bubble, a little round hope on a string. She's in the silky mood to sling that baby way on out there, her gold sleeves sliding up and down her arms. But she's got a dragon on her back, she reminds herself, and twenty self-covered buttons going across the front, on the diagonal.

Slip rounds the corner, walking jaunty, with his burlap sack on his back, just as the Baptist bells strike five. When he sees her, he takes a step backward, holds up his free hand, and says, "Whoa." He comes closer, then brings his chin in and makes his eyes go wide, pretending he's knocked off his pins, but he's also showing that a girl would have to go a lot further to get him really off balance. "The young lady I was looking for wasn't wearing no goddess outfit. When last seen she was more the ready-for-action type."

"I'm ready for action," speaks up Undella, tossing her hair, then blushes at the bold, laughing way he takes her words.

But then he sets down his burlap sack by the wall and catches hold of the front brim of his hat and brings it down a notch, to show it's time to get serious. "Well then, let's begin, Stony. Because there's worlds to learn and every bit of it begins in the wrist." He lays a thumb on the underneath of her hand and a slim brown finger over the top of it, so as to snap her wrist up and down, up and down, then turns it over and bends it backward. "This is the secret of all yo-yo motion," he explains, his long face serious, "L-O-V-E" written across his four finger bones. Where his black shirt cuff is turned back, she can see the beginning of a tattoo on the inside of his arm—a fishtail, so it's doubtless one of those naked women at the top.

from title story of
How She Knows What She Knows About Yo-Yos

Rosa had sat at that window for a long time, her hands on the wide sill, enjoying herself. The bells of the old church rang out eleven times, but still small children ran around. A man with a short white pony was giving rides around the square. He had a red scarf tied around his neck, and the pony had one, too, to match. Rosa still remembered one child, a girl, four or five years old, in a yellow dress and bright blue tights. As the man lifted her down from the pony, he swung her around and around; her little blue legs flew out, she screamed a high, excited scream.

Rosa had sat there at the window until she heard Gilbert's key in the lock. Then she pulled the curtains together and lay down on the bed with her eyes closed. She didn't want to hear what happened in the bar. She didn't want to tell him about the little girl—it would just turn into one of his stories. She lay beside him with her eyes closed, listening to the song playing over and over. She lay still and breathed in and out.

Ten, fifteen years ago, that was. That girl would be a young woman by now.

The bourbon had made Rosa lightheaded. Her body seemed to float upward, away from her bones, to turn as the room was turning, in sliding circles. She switched off the lamp and laid her head back carefully on the pillow. No breath in this room now but her own. She stared for a minute into the empty sliding darkness, then closed her eyes against it. Something still turned like a slow Ferris wheel behind her eyes. It made her feel sick. To take her mind off it, she remembered—just in her head, not out loud—that sweet melody from the movie house. The white pony. The little girl in blue stockings, swinging out, swinging out, screaming for joy.

from "Banana Boats"
How She Knows What She Knows About Yo-Yos

afterword

From the age of eleven through sixteen I worked for a commercial photographer—a second cousin on my mother's side—out on shoots and in the darkroom, ten hours a day and sometimes more when I wasn't in school, and as many as possible when I was, until ball-playing took me over. Our principal account was with the University of Kentucky Athletics Department, making publicity pictures and game stills, and films of some of the big games, before game-films were commonplace. Given UK's prominence in basketball, the account got us an occasional assignment from national magazines, and credits otherwise out of our league. I began my press-pass days in 1946 with a 3 1/4 x 4 1/4 Speed Graphic, tracking Adolph Rupp's NIT championship team, and then in 1948 his famous "Fabulous Five" NCAA champions, back when the home games were played in tiny Alumni Gym, which seated 3000 on bleachers that were folded down from the wall a few hours before tipoff, and back up as soon as the crowd was out, readying the gym for PE classes and intramural sports the next day. And I ended my press-pass days with Bear Bryant's Sugar Bowl Championship football team of 1951, up from 3 1/4 to 4 x 5, and not only on the sidelines or in the press box at games, but in closed practices too sometimes. This was a Golden Era in college sports, especially bright and buoyant for a country emerging from the dark heaviness of WWII. Rupp and Bryant at the same school—for as long as the Baron would put up with the competition, or the Bear could stand not being the biggest deal: it carried sports-loving Lexington into the Promised Land.

Only three or four photographers were allowed courtside in Alumni Gym, and kept in the corners, not quite out of harm's way on that tiny floor, but close. To be among them, and just a kid, well...I need to get this lined up just right. I was a kind of orphan, I needed a lot of help, and being that close to my heroes, to such celebrities, fed me where I was starved. The camera became one of my spirits, and later one of my guides, as did language in due course. Ralph Beard and Alex Groza from basketball, and all their teammates, Babe Parelli and Bob Gain from football, and all theirs, these All-Americans lived in the pre-TV imaginations of sports fans across the state and nationwide via the images we made of them—voiced over at home, let me hasten to add, by the radio play-by-play, and by newspaper and magazine stories.

There wasn't enough light to shoot movie film in Alumni Gym; all the basketball films were of road games. Football game films were shot from atop the press box at the fifty-yard-line, a roof and free hot-dogs and a half-time stat-sheet our only amenities: a 100' hand-wound Bell and Howell with a fixed focal-length 25mm lens, and a viewfinder as hard to read at that distance as the wrong end of a tel-escope—two of them, workhorses of the industry at the time, on tripods. While I was reloading and marking cans, I called out where the ball was going, helping the boss track the play. After the game we packaged the film in the car, with the '46 Chevy heater warming up too slowly, and took the package to the Greyhound station; on Tuesday when it came back from the lab Special Delivery via the Postal Service, I was out of school and waiting, with the help of a writ-ten note from my guardian. Splicing eleven or twelve 100' rolls into a continuous action with the help of a viewer, I was the first person to see each of those films (something I seem to have been waiting fifty plus years to get into the record). With a great private ceremony I put the big brown 16mm reel I'd just created into a big brown 16mm can, where it fit perfectly, as only a few things did, and with black paint and a small brush wrote UK vs. Temple and the date on the side, and ran a strip of one-inch white adhesive tape around the circumfer-ence. If the boss was out on a job, I got to pedal the awaited film of Saturday's game over to campus one-armed, a show-off's dream but without an audience.

When the season was over, and the coaches were done with them, those early game films came back to the studio, and we rent-ed them out to American Legion Posts and Kiwanis Clubs and Chambers of Commerce around the state, often with me attached, aged eleven, twelve, thirteen, to call the play-by-play over the pro-jector mike. In the windowless supply room, I practiced my commen-tary with the help of the twenty-three-year-old secretary, during breaks in front office business. The only thing that bored her more than basketball and football games was motion pictures of them, but she cared about me, and knew that I was hurt and heart-sick just on the other side of my good manners, my industry and precociousness, desperate for someone to pay attention to me, especially a woman, since all the men were such duds.

"You're good," she'd say several times during a half-hour prac-tice session. "Talk a little slower," she told me, or "a little louder." If I was accompanying the UK-Temple basketball game for a screening in Hazard or Corbin, usually a driver was sent to Lexington for me, but several times I went by Greyhound, and always looked forward to her taking me to the station, and hanging around until the bus pulled out, smiling and waving. Maybe she never threw a kiss even once, but you'll never get me to believe it.

A family scandal turned tragic had what was left of the Halls in a shell-shocked shambles, with me and my older sister living with our beloved paternal grandmother. Though we used to have a big house with servants and didn't any more, though we used to look like a prominent family, and didn't any more, hardly like a family at all, though the list of things that couldn't be talked about was long, and included my mother, we acted nonetheless as though nothing had happened. I was too young to know that it was acting. With my memory locked up inside the violence of my mother's suicide, and inside the silence that surrounded it like an armed force, I grew up not knowing what story I was in, and continued not to know for years, even after I was an often-autobiographical story-writer in his mid-years. I was fixed in an innocence that paralyzed my heart and imag-ination, that held my soul's progress in hock. That held shame off, or more exactly tried to, at far too great a cost. These very words are yet another effort to untie my tongue, to get the light circulating again, to use my penny on the blown fuse.

My Granny loved me, and was looking after me the very best she could, that's all I was sure of, growing up, that and the fact she was getting old and infirm, that we were using up the money. Nailed to the tree in the tiny front yard was a hand-painted sign advertising developing and printing for 35 cents a roll, covered with starling droppings in season; every morning before I went to school or work, I delivered a paper route. I rode my bicycle a few blocks home from work at lunch, and with my peanut butter and mayonnaise sandwich and milk in my favorite glass, I pulled the curtains in Granny's parlor, and lying on the couch with my eyes closed, listened to Bloody Mary's beautifully lonely voice singing "Bali Hai" from *South Pacific*. *Most people live on a lonely island, lost in the middle of a foggy sea.* Being lonely wasn't any fun, but being alone was, for my soul could come out of hiding. The darkroom was the perfect place, nobody could enter without my permission.

Photographs are ghosts, even more obviously than words—you take them for less, or for granted, at your peril. What have I done in my life more breathtakingly instructive than to look at a photograph, any photograph, when I'm up to it? Now and then, here and there, you and I, present and absent, many primary coordinates of our daytime lives are called into question, I can no longer tell the conjure from the conjurer, the face from the no-face. I get a little hit of eternity, of elsewhere, right in the quick of here and now, no division, and the world as I have always known it slows way down, pauses. Out of the frame comes to me something from a great distance, not so ordinary as I ordinarily think, Mary Ann age six still among us. I'm among the gods, as she is, present at the creation. The experience is so subversive, the stakes so high, I'm unable to rise to the occasion often or stay for long, except to remember that while I'm there, I can spit into the swinging jug—as close to enlightenment as I'm likely to get.

Most days during those early years in photography, I went home from the studio only to eat and sleep, and sometimes not even to sleep, staying on the green vinyl couch in the outer office, my paper-route bags for a pillow. A lot of the time that's what it took to get the privacy I needed to work on my art photographs. I dared not let the boss see how much paper I used, trying to get a perfect print. And I didn't want anybody questioning my choice of subjects, or asking me what I was going to do with the pictures, once I got them just right. I slipped my single-weight glossy 8x10 Kodabromides, and my double-weight Opal G's, out of the studio as though I were stealing something, and snuck them into my room upstairs at Granny's house as though they were dirty pictures. I kept them hidden, mostly, except to send them in to contests, and out for juried exhibitions. My father, who came to visit occasionally, would want me to think that I was wasting my time and money, my sister wanted to keep her distance, but Granny Hall, if everything was lined up just right for both of us, she would deal with her bifocals and look at a few of my pictures.

"What's this one of?" she asked when she couldn't find a person to look at.

"That's the three hundred block of Catalpa. I just liked the way it looked."

"How did you get way out there?"

"On my motorbike."

"I want you to be careful now. You'll make me sorry I ever let you have that thing, if you get hurt."

She was sitting in her easy chair next to the window, her crocheting in her hands, her hands in her lap, her glasses in need of cleaning, most likely, a roll of Tums within reach. She had a great soft lap and bosom, she smelled of talcum powder. I was straddling her yarn and the wicker basket with the unraveling ball in it, showing off my next one, a horse's head in silhouette, always hopeful that maybe someday...what? Our lives wouldn't be so full of such silence.

"You're getting to be quite the little picture man. I'll say that for you," she'd say, signaling that she'd seen enough.

In the supply room at work was a stash of my boss's abandoned art photography magazines: show catalogs, Photographic Society of America journals and annuals, assorted contest issues of *Popular Photography* and *U.S. Camera*, and the like. I wouldn't get them out if I had to worry about someone asking me what I was doing, or worse, coming over and sitting down and looking over my shoulder. Or even worse, commenting. An angel had come down and cast a spell over me, touching my eyes especially, conferring a lot. An exuberant peace, a joy, a dream, a spell, a grand life to buoy my small one. A clutch of charms, a store of treasures. My favorite pictures, I kept them set aside, careful not to look if I wasn't worthy, or to look too often. I loved the bio notes of the artists, and remembered a lot of what I read there. I loved to go back through my non-favorites time and again, enchanted by the world of the PSA-sanctioned salons. The 1948 Minneapolis Salon of Photography, The 1950 Boston International. You submitted four mounted prints, you got a sticker to go on the back of the mount of an accepted picture, your name in a catalog, maybe even your work reproduced.

238

The foul-weather Chesapeake Bay seascapes of A. Aubrey Bodine, FPSA, created great longing in me, a kind of heartache. Longing for what exactly I had no idea, except all those initials after my name. Well, that wasn't altogether true—I longed for things disappearing into a fog, or trying to emerge out of it, the same longing I felt listening to *South Pacific*, and Ezio Pinza singing about enchantment, "Once you have found her, never let her go." Or reading Edgar Allan Poe, my only literary experience before college. Longing for life in that part of the mind, where trance was possible, and dream much more real than the actual world it left behind. Longed for depth, beauty, holiness, staying-power, for the stirrings of my soul, for the spunk to live with my fears and my shame. For what I was finding in art.

My first sightings of Alfred Stieglitz's cloud pictures and his portraits of O'Keefe, of Edward Weston's Lobos rocks, his peppers and nudes, of Ansel Adams's Yosemite, and Henri Cartier-Bresson's Paris were made sitting cross-legged on the cool cement floor of the supplyroom after everyone else was gone. My introduction to Stieglitz's *Camera Work*, and the campaign he waged for photography in the art world, took place under a #2 flood brought in from the front room, after I'd gone home to eat and come back to be alone there some more. Minor White's nature abstractions were among my treasures, though I wasn't at all sure I should be liking those runes as much as I did—wasn't I isolated enough already?

The secretary, whose name I cannot remember but whose skin I can still touch, was the only friend I had in those early intensities. A sultry high-school graduate with large lidded eyes and luscious lips, indifferent to the life of the mind, she wasn't at all interested in the twenty-eight-year-old in-house stud, and the boss was no competition at all. I was newly pubescent, but I had an old soul, maybe that was it—something made it possible for me to pull a chair up next to hers and touch her lightly on the forearm during conversation.

When the odds favored our privacy, sometimes I showed her some of my treasures. Five or six or seven at a showing, from different magazines and catalogs, the places marked with black separation papers from 4 x 5 sheet film, folded longways once. She crossed her arms under her breasts, and moved around to where she could look straight at the Bodine oyster-dredging I was holding out for her to look at. I wouldn't say anything. I held a picture out between us for what I felt was the right amount of time, and went to the next one. When she began working a cigarette out of her pack, that was a good sign. Usually she had a favorite, or two.

"The moon one," she said once when a show was over.

I knew which one she was talking about—it wasn't as obvious as it sounds—and was thrilled, all over my body, my soul and groin oscillating. It was one of my favorites too, a Minor White...what a strange name, Minor! We looked at this secret again, as though we'd crawled into a cave together, or was it out onto a rock shelf in the moonlight, in full view of eternity and...what else was it out there in there down there over there? How do you talk about these experiences, except by throwing some words at a moving target that never leaves its place? In full view of the mother, many mothers, maybe all of them, where there is no shame. The bio note, I searched it out, and read it to her, as she was lighting up.

Then—if it wasn't then, it ought to have been, and is now for the record—I showed her "Perpetual Motion," my prize-winning picture in the latest issue of *U.S. Camera*. We were long seconds into looking at it, when I realized that she might not know what perpetual meant. Nor that the picture was mine. I hadn't told anyone, I didn't want to be conceited. She might never know, the credit line wasn't bold enough, and I was helpless to think of any way to make sure that she did—without sounding like I had the big-head, or was soliciting praise. I might never have known that she knew I was the artist had she not said later on, "You know more big words than a kid your age has got any business knowing," which thrilled me every bit as much as, and was indistinguishable from, a response to my picture.

Sometimes my treasure required that I pull the chair up next to her, sometimes she leaned over toward me...close enough for the outsides of our thighs to be pressing up against each other. We were both about 5'6," I weighed probably 120, she 135. Usually she was perfumed. She had brown hair, always freshly washed, smoked Lucky Strikes that she kept in a pack-sized plastic case, often on the desk in front of her, with a silver Zippo on top. For music she carried a small green transistor radio, the latest thing, turned way down and hidden so that she could get it turned off if the boss was imminent. At some point I probably asked her if I could stroke her leg, though I may have just started doing it, along the top, a little more confidently each day, until I was down on the inside—all this taking place under the cover of my darkroom apron. Soon I had my quivering hand under her skirt, first along the outside of her shaved, tanned thigh, oh-my-god, and then after a week or two of wordless negotiation, along the inside, far enough up to feel the inside of her other thigh, moist on the back of my hand, with her answering the phone and lighting cigarettes and going about her secretarial duties as necessary. At any given time I knew exactly where the boundaries were, and when they might be open to renegotiation, though neither of us ever said a word, even when I got her skirt far enough up once along her outside thigh to see that her panties were a pale yellow. I had wanted them to be pink, but what's a little disappointment between intimates?

Finally I asked her. "Can I take your picture?"

For too long she didn't say anything, looking at all ten of her up-pointing fingernails, and then just the right-hand five turned inside out and down, until I was thinking I'd made a mistake, and that maybe she thought I meant nude, though I'd been too timid to include any nudes in what I showed her, or for that matter among my private favorites. "Sure," she said finally, never looking at me. Afterwards I thought a lot about her not looking at me, and maybe thinking I meant nude, which filled me one breath with anticipation and dance steps, and the next with alibis and dread.

After the shop closed one spring night, and I was sure no one was coming back, we made a cashmere sweater portrait of her with her stomach sucked in, to give to her boyfriend, who'd never before been mentioned.

Before she left, I got her to release the shutter on the chin-in-hands self-portrait shown here, one of two negatives that has survived the fifty plus years, the other being "Perpetual Motion," a night-time long-exposure shot of cars flowing like an s-curved river of light down an expressway and under an overpass.

Twenty-five years to the season and probably the month after I read the bio note of Minor White to the secretary on High Street near Woodland in Lexington, Kentucky, I was sitting with him in his backyard in Arlington, Massachusetts, listening to him talk about his life, and the life of the Milky Way, which was especially vivid overhead that night. My fiction writing was on hold, my poetry writing just beginning, and I was back doing art photography, for the first time really as an adult. Though I was teaching a "Words and Pictures" course in his Creative Photography Department at MIT, and working with him as a Contributing Editor for his magazine *Aperture: the Quarterly of Photography*, the successor to Stieglitz's *Camera Work*, I was there that evening in the new role of his chosen biographer. Talking to Minor often involved long silences, that put into their this-world place all the words your karma had caused you to commit. We were in the middle of one, both staring up at the heavens, when I remembered for the first time in years and years the nameless secretary and the insides of her steamy thighs and the showing of "the moon one." I had to stifle laughter, overcome incredulity, hold back tears. I had to promise myself that I'd return to the moment when I had the time and the strength of spirit to do it justice. All of which I'd forgotten until I set out here to track my beginnings in photography, that first episode in the story of becoming an artist. It's a journey that can't be fully accounted for without reference to a woman's skin and a woman's heat, which have been present all along the way.

Several times since then I've had experiences similar to the one with Minor White and the Milky Way: of my messy, chaotic fog-bound life being revealed to me, however momentarily, in its underlying coherence and clarity, even comeliness, in its state of grace, where my shame has no place. And each time art has been the agent. This may be art's deepest charge, to release us from the prison of our hurts and move us beyond complaint. Not the next such experience or the next, but maybe the one after that occurred in 1995, when the UK Art Museum exhibited my *Orphan in the Attic* photographs, which told the dark story, finally, of Lurlene Bronough, a beauty queen on the campus during the 20s, marrying into the Hall family, and of my buried childhood. The story I'd sent my lenses in and amongst the family albums to dig up and sort out, my language to test and verify, back and forth, and vice versa, remembering without the aid of memory. Like Stieglitz, Weston and Mark Rothko, like Rainer Maria Rilke, T.S. Eliot, W.S.Merwin and Louise Glück—in the swiftest current of art's deepest trough.

And it's happening now again, with *A Spring-Fed Pond: My Friendships with Five Famous American Writers Over the Years*, a book and an exhibition celebrating some of my All-American artist friends, from the happier side of my life, from what's proud in our culture and my heritage. When I notice that the Singletary Center for the Arts is where Stoll Field used to be, Rose at Euclid, and the UK Art Museum where the old press box used to be—the hot dogs replaced by hors d'oeuvres at the opening, the half-time stats by this book—I'm of a mind to notice also that two buildings away, in the Library's Special Collections, those early game films are close by to the accumulating papers of the writers pictured here. And as Merwin says, I bow, "not knowing to what."